THE PLANT LIFE CYCLE

by Arnold Ringstad

The Child's World
childsworld.com

Published by The Child's World®
1980 Lookout Drive • Mankato, MN 56003-1705
800-599-READ • www.childsworld.com

Photographs ©: Shutterstock Images, cover (foreground), cover (background), 1 (foreground), 1 (background), 6, 13, 14, 18; Brian A. Jackson/Shutterstock Images, 5; Jack Hong/Shutterstock Images, 9; Blue Ring Media/Shutterstock Images, 10; iStockphoto, 17; Kazakova Maryia/Shutterstock Images, 20 (dandelions and background); Viktorija Reuta/Shutterstock Images, 20 (bee)

ISBN 9781503828476
LCCN 2018944816

Printed in the United States of America
PA02396

About the Author

Arnold Ringstad has written more than 70 books for students. He especially enjoys reading and writing about space exploration. Ringstad lives in Minnesota with his wife and their cat.

Table of Contents

CHAPTER ONE

From Seed to Plant

It is a warm summer day. The wind carries away seeds from a dandelion. They float through the air like small parachutes. They settle on the ground. Some will grow roots in the dirt. Water and sunshine will help them grow. Then they will become new dandelion plants. This process is part of the plant life cycle.

Plants are important to life on Earth. Some provide food for people. Vegetables and fruits are plants. People need these plants for a healthy diet. Animals eat plants, too. They wouldn't be able to grow without plants. Some people eat animals, too.

One dandelion can have between 54 and 172 seeds.

Plants have other uses, too. Wood comes from trees. People burn wood for heat. Scientists use plants to make medicines. For example, aloe gel is often used to treat sunburns. It comes from an aloe vera plant. Many kinds of clothing are made from cotton. Cotton is a plant. Plants also release a gas called oxygen into the **atmosphere**. People and animals need oxygen to breathe.

Plants go through a life cycle. The cycle creates new plants. It allows the plants to survive and spread. This cycle makes life as we know it possible.

People have been using juice from the aloe vera plant for thousands of years.

CHAPTER TWO

Pollen and Seeds

New plants are made in the first part of the plant life cycle. This part of the cycle includes three stages. The first is pollination. Next comes fertilization. The last stage is dispersal.

Pollination involves a material called **pollen**. This is a sticky, powdery material. It is produced in the male part of the flower, called the stamen. Pollen contains tiny grains. Pollination happens when these grains move from one flower to another of the same kind. But pollen cannot travel by itself. It has to be carried.

A **vector** brings pollen from one flower to another. A vector is anything that can move pollen. It may be blowing wind or flowing water. It may be a bird, insect, or bat. An animal that carries pollen is called a **pollinator**. Pollinators often feed on flowers. While they are there, the pollen sticks to them. The pollinator carries pollen to the next flower it feeds on.

Bees frequently pollinate flowers.

Parts of a Flower

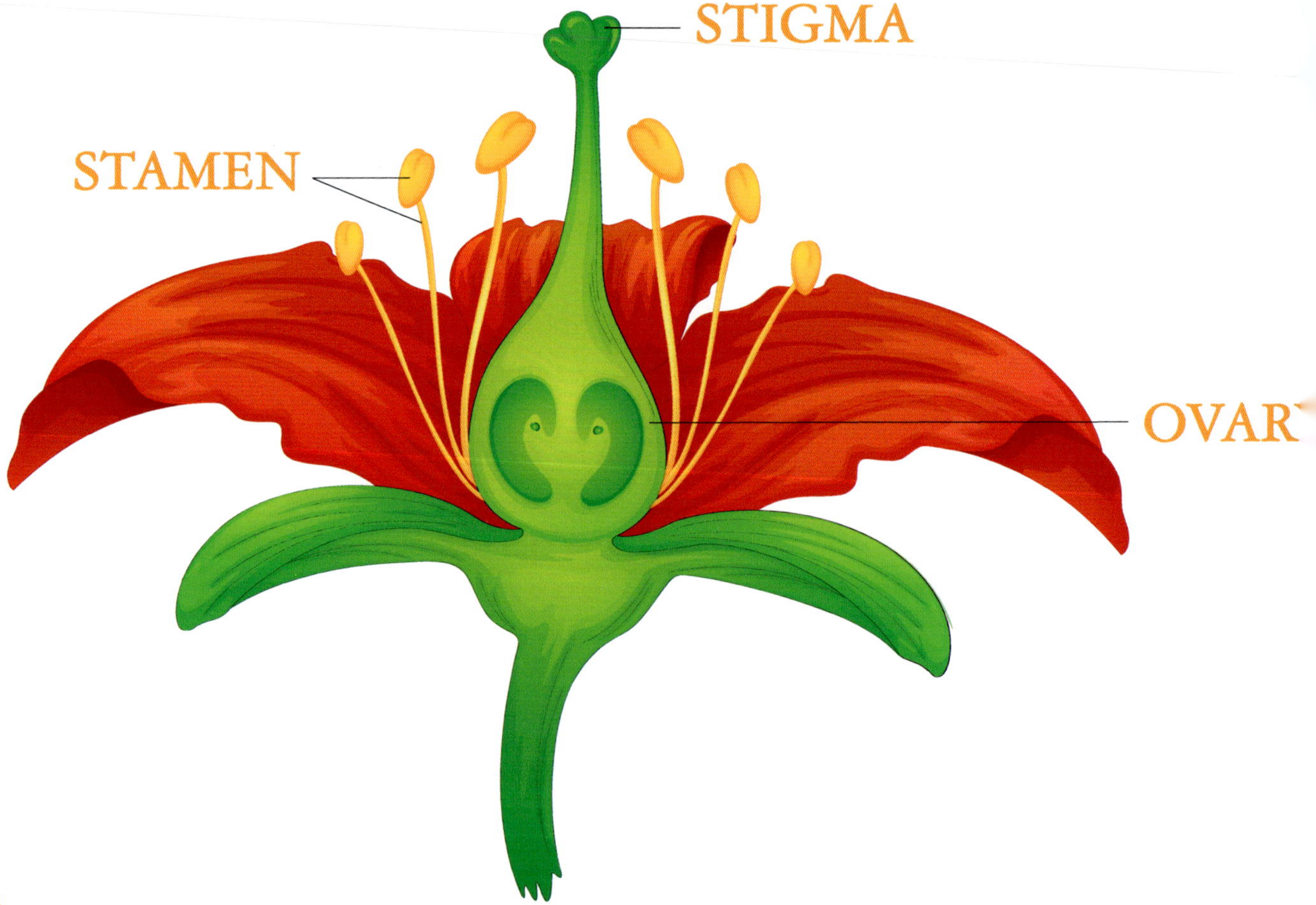

Fertilization happens after pollen reaches a new flower. The pollen is collected at the **stigma**. The pollen travels down into the plant's ovary. Here, the pollen grains can develop into seeds. In some plants, a fruit or a pod grows around the seed. This helps protect the seed.

Dispersal happens after the seeds form. They are carried to a new place by a vector. For dandelions, wind is the vector. It carries the floating seeds away. Some plants use water as a vector. A flowing river can carry the seeds downstream. The seeds may end up at a distant riverbank. Animals also help move seeds. For example, some seeds stick to an animal's fur. This can carry the seeds to a new place.

A flower's stamen, stigma, and ovary are essential to the plant life cycle.

CHAPTER THREE

Growing and Maturing

Once a plant's seed has arrived in its new spot, the next step is germination. This process happens when the seed breaks open. Roots grow from the seed into the ground. The roots absorb water and nutrients. The growing plant needs sunlight and warm temperatures, too.

The plant's shoot rises up and out of the ground. After the shoot grows some more, it is known as the stem. Leaves grow from the stem. The plant keeps getting larger. It grows until it is **mature**. A mature plant is ready to **reproduce**. It grows flowers, and these flowers produce pollen. The whole cycle starts over again.

Seeds can only germinate if they have healthy soil.

Growing Seasons

The length of a plant's life cycle depends on the type of plant. Some plants are called annuals. It takes them one year to complete a life cycle. Some plants are called biennials. It takes them two years to complete one life cycle. Some plants can live longer than either annuals or biennials. They are called perennials. Peonies are an example of a perennial. They can live up to 100 years.

While a plant is alive, it performs **photosynthesis**. In this process, the plant takes in water, sunlight, and a gas called carbon dioxide. It uses these to make food for itself. The process also gives off oxygen.

All plants eventually die. They might not get enough water or sun. Another plant nearby might use up important nutrients. A fire might sweep through an area. When plants die, they **decompose**. They break apart and release nutrients back into the soil. This can help other plants grow.

Peonies can grow back every spring for many years.

CHAPTER FOUR

Pollution and Plants

Pollution can harm plants in many ways. Sometimes it can kill plants. In other cases, it can disrupt the plant life cycle.

Some plants grow underwater. They are found in lakes or oceans. Pollution on the water's surface can block sunlight. Without sunlight, photosynthesis slows down. The plants can't produce food, so they can't grow.

Most cars give off air pollution when they are driven. This pollution can harm plants. Scientists know that pollution can delay plants from creating flowers. This disrupts the plants' life cycle.

Fumes from cars can hurt the environment.

ONLY
ONLY

Pollution in the soil can harm a plant's roots. The roots are not able to take in as many nutrients. Without these nutrients, the plant's growth slows down.

Plants are important to life on Earth. They help people create food, energy, and air to breathe. A danger to them is a danger to all living things. Helping them complete their life cycles can help keep our planet healthy.

Picking up trash can benefit both animals and plants.

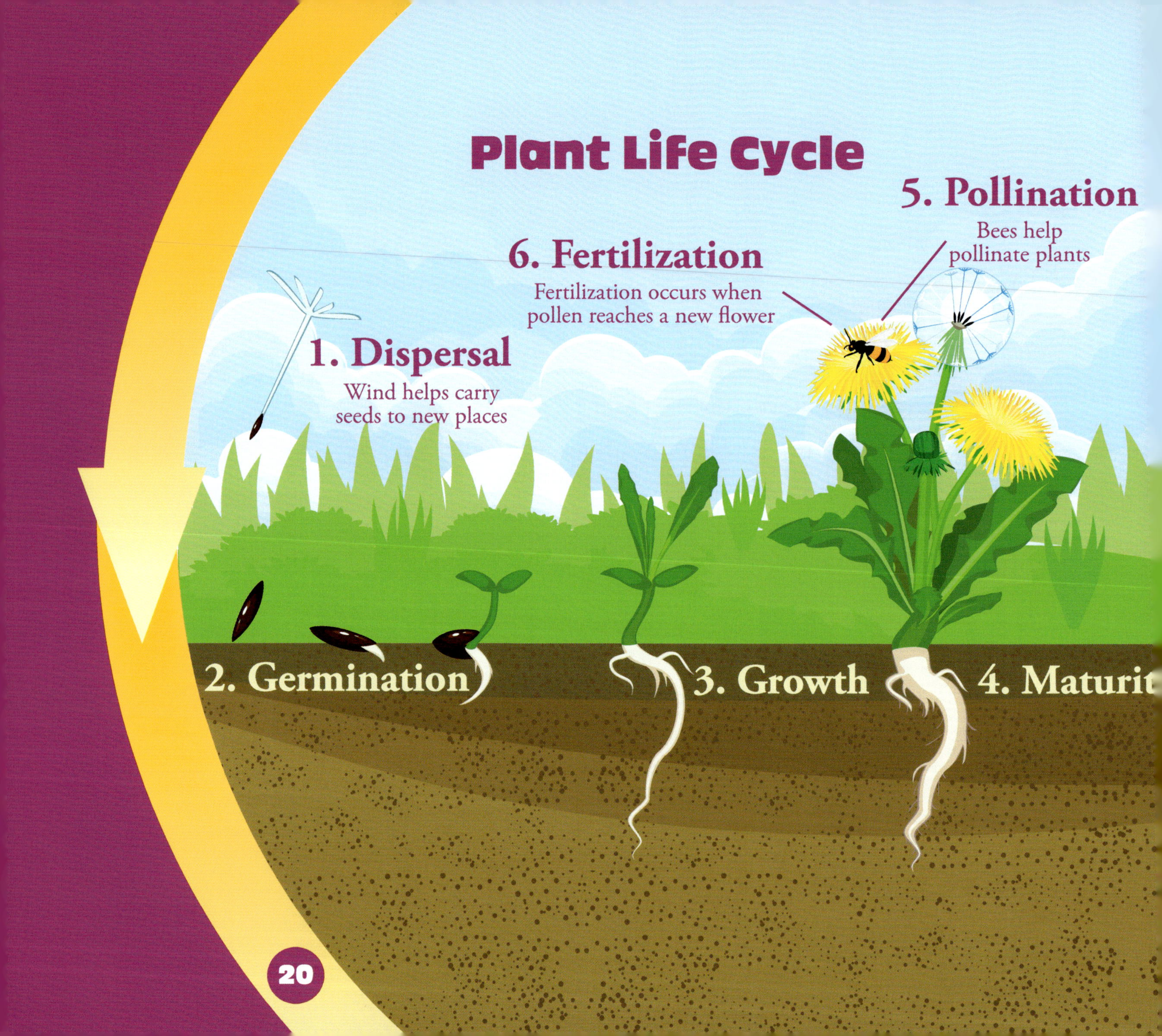
Plant Life Cycle
5. Pollination
Bees help pollinate plants
6. Fertilization
Fertilization occurs when pollen reaches a new flower
1. Dispersal
Wind helps carry seeds to new places
2. Germination
3. Growth
4. Maturit

Fast Facts

- Plants provide food, energy, and air to breathe.
- Vectors may carry pollen from one plant to another.
- Through the fertilization process, the pollen becomes a new plant seed.
- In the dispersal step, the seed is carried to a new location.
- When a seed germinates, it creates roots and begins to grow.
- After plants grow and mature, they are able to reproduce. The cycle begins again.
- Pollution can disrupt the plant life cycle.

Glossary

atmosphere (AT-muhs-feer) The atmosphere is the gases surrounding Earth. Plants release oxygen into the atmosphere.

decompose (dee-kuhm-POZE) To decompose is to break down after death. Plants decompose after they die.

mature (muh-CHUR) To mature is to have grown enough to be able to reproduce. Plants grow until they are mature.

photosynthesis (foh-toh-SIN-thi-sis) Photosynthesis is the process by which a plant uses sunlight to change water and carbon dioxide into food for itself. Plants can perform photosynthesis.

pollen (PAH-luhn) Pollen is a powdery material that plants use to reproduce. Pollen can be carried from plant to plant by animals.

pollinator (PAH-luh-nay-tur) A pollinator is an animal that carries pollen from plant to plant. A bee can be a pollinator.

pollution (puh-LOO-shun) Pollution is a harmful substance that is released into the environment. Pollution can harm the plant life cycle.

reproduce (ree-pruh-DOOS) To reproduce is to create offspring. Mature plants can reproduce.

stigma (STIG-ma) The stigma is the part of a flower that collects pollen. The stigma plays a role in seed development.

vector (VEK-tur) A vector is something that moves pollen from one place to another. Flowing water can serve as a vector.

To Learn More

IN THE LIBRARY

Duke, Shirley Smith. *Step-by-Step Experiments with Plants*. Mankato, MN: The Child's World, 2012.

Lundgren, Julie K. *Plants Make Their Own Food*. Vero Beach, FL: Rourke Pub., 2012.

Sirota, Lyn. *Insects as Pollinators*. Vero Beach, FL: Rourke Educational Media, 2016.

ON THE WEB

Visit our Web site for links about the plant life cycle:

childsworld.com/links

Note to Parents, Teachers, and Librarians: We routinely verify our Web links to make sure they are safe and active sites. So encourage your readers to check them out!

Index